W9-AMT-256

Six Legged World

THE INSECT'S BODY

Lynn M. Stone

The Rourke Book Company, Inc.
Vero Beach, Florida 32964

PHOTO CREDITS
© Lynn M. Stone: cover, title page, p. 8, 13;
© James H. Robinson: p. 4, 19;
© J. H. "Pete" Carmichael: p. 7, 11, 12, 15, 16;
© James P. Rowan: p. 20

EDITORIAL SERVICES
Janice L. Smith for Penworthy Learning Systems

Library of Congress Cataloging-in-Publication Data

Stone, Lynn M.
    The insect's body / Lynn M. Stone.
        p. cm. — (Six legged world)
    ISBN 1-55916-314-3
    1. Insects—Morphology—Juvenile literature. [1. Insects.] I. Title.

QL494 .S85 2000
595.7—dc21

00–036930

Printed in the USA

CONTENTS

The Insect's Body   5

The Head   6

The Thorax   14

The Abdomen   18

The Skeleton   21

Glossary   23

Further Reading   24

Index   24

THE INSECT'S BODY

Nature's design of an adult insect sets it apart from other animals. An insect has three main parts – a head, **thorax**, and **abdomen**. It is fairly easy to see where one section begins and ends.

The head is the first part of the body. The thorax is the middle part. The abdomen is the last section.

This red carpenter ant shows the head, thorax, and abdomen of a typical insect.

THE HEAD

The heads of most adult insects have two eyes, mouthparts, and two antennas.

The eyes of most insects are unusually large for the animal's size. Look closely at the common dragonfly, for instance. Its eyes are like little melons.

Insect antennas look like smaller models of automobile radio antennas. Some insects, such as katydids, have long, whiplike antennas. Moths have unusual, feathery antennas.

The large, compound eyes of a dragonfly are made up of thousands of individual lenses.

Insect antennas aren't for style. An insect uses its antennas to smell and touch. Some insects even use their antennas as taste testers and hearing aids. An insect without its antennas is nearly helpless.

An insect's mouth is just an opening to its head. The **mouthparts** around the mouth do the biting, chewing, and piercing.

Antennas of Polyphemus moth look like palm branches. They help the moth to smell other Polyphemus moths.

Mouthparts are much different from one insect to another. Beetles, for example, have jaw-like mouthparts. Certain bugs have long, sharp beak-like mouthparts.

Butterflies have neither jaws nor beak. Rather, butterflies and moths have a **proboscis**. The proboscis is a long, thin drinking tube.

The proboscis, like a straw, sips nectar, a sweet liquid that flowers make. A butterfly or moth can coil its proboscis up like a rope when it's not in use.

Bess beetle has sharp, clawlike mouthparts for holding prey.

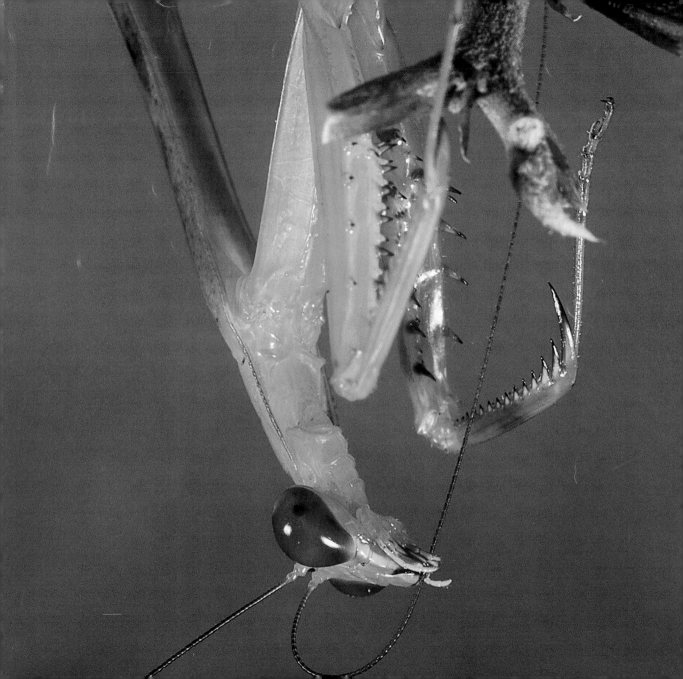

*The shiny exoskeleton of a stinkbug is light
and strong.*

This cecropia moth caterpillar has chewing mouthparts. As an adult, it will not eat, nor have chewing mouthparts.

13

THE THORAX

The thorax holds muscles that operate an insect's wings and legs. The wings and legs are attached to the outside of the thorax.

An adult insect has three pairs of legs. Each leg is divided into five main sections.

Wings and legs of an insect, like this cicada killer wasp, are attached to the animal's thorax.

Just as mouthparts differ, so do legs. Insect legs are designed to help an insect survive in its own **niche**. A niche is the special place in nature where an animal best fits. Locusts, for example, have long, powerful rear legs for jumping in grass.

Insects are the only cold-blooded animals with wings. Insects have either two wings, four wings, or no wings at all.

The most well-known four-winged insects are moths, butterflies, and dragonflies. Common houseflies are among the two-winged insects.

Long, spiky legs of a praying mantis can grasp and hold the insects that the mantis eats.

THE ABDOMEN

The abdomen contains most of an insect's soft internal organs. An insect's organs keep its body running properly.

Many insects have a pair of tiny, clawlike feelers at the end of their abdomens. The feelers are used as weapons.

The abdomen of many female insects has an **ovipositor**. The ovipositor is a long, slim tool for laying eggs.

The earwig's abdomen has sharp feelers, or pincers, used for grabbing prey and for defense.

THE SKELETON

Insects don't have bones, but they do have a skeleton, an **exoskeleton**.

An exoskeleton is on the outside rather than the inside. An insect's exoskeleton is made of chitin. Chitin is lighter and stronger than bone.

The muscles of an insect are attached to the inside wall of its chitin exoskeleton. The skeleton covers an adult insect like a hard, plastic jacket.

This katydid molts out of its old exoskeleton and leaves it behind.

The exoskeleton consists of ringlike sections. Some of the rings are molded together. Others are attached by stretchy material.

Every so often a growing insect sheds its exoskeleton like an old coat. This process is called **molting**. A new, larger exoskeleton takes the place of the old one.

GLOSSARY

abdomen (AB duh men) — the last section of an insect's body, where most of its organs are

exoskeleton (EK so SKEH luh tun) — a firm, supporting structure (skeleton) on the outside of an animal

mouthparts (MOUTH pahrts) — the jaws, beak, or other feeding tools that surround an insect's mouth

molting (MOLT ing) — the replacement of an outer covering by a new, larger covering

niche (NITSH) — a special place into which each plant and animal fits in nature

ovipositor (O vuh pah zuh tur) — a long, slender tube which a female insect uses to deposit her eggs

proboscis (pruh BAH sus) — the long, strawlike tube used by moths and butterflies to drink nectar from flowers

thorax (THAWR aks) — the middle section of an insect, where its wings and six legs are attached

FURTHER READING

Find out more about the bodies of insects and insects in general with these helpful books and information sites:

- Everts, Tammy and Kalman, Bobbie. *Bugs and Other Insects.* Crabtree, 1994
- Green, Jen. *Learn About Insects.* Lorenz, 1998
- Parker, Steve. *Insects.* Dorling Kindersley, 1992
- Stone, Lynn M. *What Makes an Insect?* Rourke, 1997

Wonderful World of Insects on-line at www.insect-world.com

INDEX

abdomen 5, 18
antennas 6, 9
beetles 10
butterflies 10, 17
chitin 21
dragonfly 6, 17
eyes 6
exoskeleton 21, 22

feelers 18
head 5, 6
insects 5, 6, 9, 10, 14, 17, 18, 21, 22
  niche of 17
legs 14, 17
mouth 9
mouthparts 6, 9, 10, 17

muscles 14, 21
nectar 10
organs 18
ovipositor 18
proboscis 10
thorax 5, 14
wings 14, 17